MW00743448

CLOSER TO
WHERE WE BEGAN

CLOSER TO WHERE WE BEGAN

Lisa Richter

TIGHTROPE BOOKS

Copyright © Lisa Richter, 2017

All rights reserved. No part of this publication may be reproduced, stored in a retrieval system, or transmitted, in any form or by any means, without prior permission of the publisher or, in the case of photocopying or other reprographic copying, a licence from Access Copyright, the Canadian Copyright Licensing Agency. www.accesscopyright.ca, info@accesscopyright. Printed in Canada.

Tightrope Books
#207-2 College Street,
Toronto Ontario, Canada M5G 1K3
tightropebooks.com
bookinfo@tightropebooks.com

EDITOR: Jacob Scheier
COPYEDITOR: Heather Wood
COVER IMAGE: Janice Colman
COVER & LAYOUT DESIGN: David Jang

Produced with the assistance of the Canada Council for the Arts and the Ontario Arts Council.

Library and Archives Canada Cataloguing in Publication

Richter, Lisa, 1977-, author
        Closer to where we began / Lisa Richter.

Poems.
ISBN 978-1-988040-18-9 (softcover)

        I. Title.

PS8635.I3485C56 2017   C811'.6   C2017-900681-9

To the memory of my grandparents
Florence & Philip Colman
Chana & Joseph Richter
my step-grandmother, Bella

and most of all to Stéphane

sometimes I can feel it, the way we are
pouring slowly toward a curve and around it
through something dark and soft, and we are bound
to each other.
—Sharon Olds

Table of Contents

I

II

III

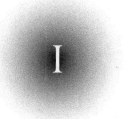

I

Inscription

At your father's beach house near Shediac,
the air tastes of rock salt, smoked
fish. Seaweed drapes over rocks, emerald wigs
on Styrofoam mannequin busts. Indigo and turquoise
bottle glass blinds us in morning sun
as the messages they once held
wash out into white noise and foam.
A siege of herons elongate their bodies
from grounded commas into airborne
dashes—the words from blacked-out texts
the wind redacts. You point out
Prince Edward Island, strip of blue-grey
gauze stretched over the horizon's mouth.
The ocean recedes for miles. Patches
of wet sand gleam with bald stones, fragments
of oyster shell, whelk and mollusk. Hermit crabs skulk
in blood-warm lagoons that will widen
and deepen when it's time to turn back,
forcing new routes and detours
through weedy, rippling pools, the land
these effacing tides subtract. Stretches
of beach un-scroll, inscribed with the memory
of our walking, this early September day,
our blowing dark hair, your hand
on my hip a scallop shell, fanning outward,
as we get closer to where we began.

Stripping for Rilke

When her soul oozed out of her skin, bleeding
like a ghost of ink, my mouth stretched wide

to catch its melt—that February day
in Montreal, in the bookstore on Milton, she stripped

away layers of ice-damp wool, casting off
the heavy skins of winter, and a pale bare arm

emerged, scattering freckles like grains of wild rice
and reaching past my amber face for Rilke's

Duino Elegies she raised her gentle voice
and read: "*Every angel is terrible, and still,*

alas knowing all that, I serenade you, you almost
deadly birds of the soul."

Breakfast with My Doppelganger

How awkward it is: the teething
of butter-knives,
      uneven slurps of coffee,

our handling of silverware demanding
displays of similar posture. The way
we hold our mugs in both hands

and blow across the surface, the staggered
ripples of our breath tipping
the liquid's edge. It is like watching

myself in a mirror, only different,
because I do not know
      where to look, where not to,
or what for. My doppelganger

stares back over the burnt
toast's charred crust.
      Her eyes dark like mine.
        Her gaze darker.

It Was Not an Apple

she ate but a blood orange,
whose burgundy juice chanted dark requiems
to her sun-brushed breasts
and baked clay thighs,

which sang of knowledge
not yet arcane, jelly of quivering cells,
foretelling ice, flint, flame, mushrooms sprouting
in early cattle dung.

To unlock the fruit, she had to push
her thumbs into it, deep into chambers
hosting secret elixirs and recipes for
embalming.

When she reached the juice,
she knew she was naked
and unafraid.

What You Find in the Attic

Folded moth wings, a Morse of nostalgia beating
the muffled voices of your footsteps into submission

    five battered spiral notebooks, whose pages evoke
    forked lizard tongues, forgotten tails of tadpoles, coffee shop
    ashtrays,

    maps now golden but still crisp when unfolded, revealing the
    heart's primeval topography & routes to spangled forests, a
    thatch of roads, bouquet of spider-veins blossoming all over
    Ontario

        Mom's old Pete Seeger & Woody Guthrie albums, their jacket
        sleeves & liner notes all onion skin rustle & shimmer

photographs of old friends, the first great love you knew, that
you developed in a high school darkroom (recall how the faces
would swim up to the paper's surface

    in pomegranate juice light, from white to the clarity of black
    and silver)

        all the letters you wrote but never mailed how the past
        worms its way back into the present
                        infecting it

Ouroboros

The year I was born, my great-grandmother
died. Skimming sides and glances, we conducted
love through our bones, memory
and foreshadowing encoded in the rings

of skipped stones across drumskin-smooth
water. She wore cat's-eye glasses and a daffodil
grin, paisley polyester and wind-puffed
canvas smocks.

Her face gleamed a heavy moon white, pock-
marked with the scars of long-dried seas—
lips of calcified salt, teeth of fossilized
spine, jaw-bone, femur. They say the marbles

rolled in her head, that there, the mind lounged
and lolled. Deep in the quarry of her body
the sun-stroked fields of Belarus sang, drowning
out the traffic of Outremont life.

Once, as she danced around the Passover
table, voluminous breasts swinging, hips bumping
the backs of chairs, her feet pushed the sweet
air and she soared around the room. I too felt

the pull of Bubbe's circular laps, slipped
from my mother's arms, floated
up to join her (it took three men
over an hour to get us down).

This was how we were meant to be
acquainted: her life at the tip
of the snake's tail, mine at the apex
of its open mouth.

Fragments of Tel Aviv

i.
Midday Carmel Market sun
ties a scorching wire
around my head

a paper cup
of pomegranate juice
is cool violet light
down my throat

pulpy residue of seeds
catch on the tip of
the wave, gulp.

ii.
The shocking verve
of aquamarine
eyes, skin like papyrus

his smoky beard curling
almost pubic
to the collar of his shirt.

Black velvet *kipah*
absorbs the afternoon
sun. He cracks open

a smile with spaced
teeth, brings a joint

to his lips
and offers it to me
nodding
"*B'vakasha.*"

Please. Here.

iii.
Waiting for the
Dizengoff bus beside
an 18-year-old
with an M-16

slung over a thin
shoulder, who pushes

designer sunglasses back
over hair, laughs
into her cell phone

iv.
Motti, dreadlocked
and bare to the waist

just back from a year in Goa
after four years
in the Air Force
sits on the pier at sunset

leans into
a didgeridoo, sealing
its wooden mouth

with his, coaxes yelps
and moans from
the dark tunnel

the only sounds I ever
hear from him

v.
I ask Eyal about
the nightclubs on Allenby—

their dress codes, high cover
charges, 50-60 shekels,
some of them ages 23, 24 and up

he says *it's really to keep out
the* Arsim, *those thugs
from South Tel Aviv and Yafo*

all muscle cars and t-shirts
You wouldn't want one of them
trying to talk to you, would you?

vi.
Nadavi says: This
is frangipani, the national tree
of Laos. This is a lotus flower.

This is a *Sabras* fruit.
If you touch it, it will
prick your fingers.

This is *Datura*, a cousin
of the cannabis
family. A deadly
hallucinogen.

These are figs. They have
not ripened yet. This is
what an olive
tastes like when it's just
been picked. Here, try it.
Ha ha, you should see your
face right now. This is…

1 June 2001

i.

For all of a minute, I don't remember it,
I'm just waking to the first day
of June in Tel Aviv, a Saturday, *Shabbat*,
my one full day off, the frantic city unfurled
in weekly repose. Nearby, the *shuq*'s padlocked
metal doors cover market stalls, eyelids
drawn in willful, corrugated sleep. Then it comes back—
CNN flickers in, numbers of dead and wounded
in last night's attack embed themselves
in my ears: twenty killed, not including the bomber
himself, dozens more wounded. My roommate and I
list numbers of our own: fifteen, how many minutes
it takes to walk to the nightclub where it happened,
five, how close she was when she heard the thunder
on a clear, warm night. No numbers for the ambulances
that passed me on my way home from the Internet cafe,
no numbers for the time that passed by before
we found each other, both running towards home.
We turn off the TV and go out.

ii.

Through scalloped foliage, flowering trees
layer their scents into Mediterranean
air. The outdoor cafe servers of Neve Tsedek
dart between tables of languid brunchers, women
with bare arms sheathed in bangles sipping
cappuccinos, leaning in towards
men in sunglasses, crisp shirts open at tanned

neck. At our favourite beachside kiosk, Simon
and Garfunkel sing on the radio, *Slow down,*
you move too fast, got to make the morning last,
a sweetness that rots beneath the day's
gut-punched weight. Not far away, mourners
place flowers, others tiny stones, near the site
of the bombing, guarding against the mixing of life
with death—now the army is here,
the army is everywhere, the crowd thickens,
a pulsing thrum, veins rising in temples, some
hurling their stones at the nearest mosque.

Long Exposure

Sometime after midnight, I found our old photos
and contact sheets I thought I'd destroyed. Across the still
black lake, a loon let loose its drunken throat song, ghost
howl canoeing across stippled bay.

I scratched a mosquito bite until it bled, until the marks
of my nails were like crosses of screws stamped
into the swelling.

I poured myself another Crown Royal.

I fell asleep on the old chintz sofa, dreamed I was in a pool
front-crawling towards you as you back-stroked towards
me, only noticing as we were about to collide.

Sometime after midnight, I awoke in the creaking
cabin, beneath shadows that swam on the sloped ceiling,
where moths flickered in dim light, above blades
of a fan that stood still as the room rotated around it, blood
moon in the window, glazing
the wide-planked floor.

The night you took these pictures: red wine
in tin coffee mugs, this darkened room, my hair
still dripping with lake water, I pulled off my bathing suit
which stuck hard to my poached skin. *Hold it*, you said,
brandishing your old Nikon, and I held

everything that could be held. I remember
your hand-trails infrared on my thighs,
the weight of your tongue, its animal purpose.

You said you could never imagine
what it would be like not to know me, not to know
each other's tastes and textures, to be here.
This place we're now in.

Boxing Day

after Kenneth Koch

Along the curb of St. Urbain
running south from Mount Royal,
the unwrapped boxes lie in wait, some
already collapsed, ready for their collection,

others still holding onto
their original shape, each one
a cast-off moment
of a tree bowing its head, twisting
       its dark rings, and it's dark now

here in Montreal, like the warehouses
that once received the boxes
from a truck
       that came from a port, after being
       lifted off the loading
       dock of a ship
       that sailed from China, and

          snow's
in the forecast tonight, at last—
this year, green things groundhog up
in the blanched mud, grow cold beneath
fickle thaws, and though I love

how I can walk through this city
in December, how the numb garden plots
and I breathe in this stunted season
together, part of me still covets

the white blanketing
the world's in for, the cocooning and dreamless

sleep. My cousin Marissa reminds me
the days are getting longer now, the nights
will slowly slip into days again, and who
knows, maybe with the coming snow

I'll still get to feel it this year: the groundswell
of spring, the earth rising up to meet me
where I stand, ice cracking louder
      than the spines of cardboard boxes
      beneath a foot, broken down.

One Eye Open

For weeks we awoke to the itch of filched
blood, once-smooth bodies turned celestial maps

of bites. We scratched our Big Dippers
and Orion's Belts, which told of our defeat

in another night's campaign—how assailants
struck as we slept, crept from their foxholes

to tap our veins and steal away. Though the chemical
bombs have now been dropped, they're out

of sight but not of mind—living in the routine
of vacuuming every inch of carpet, drying bedding

and clothes on maximum heat, the invisible sandbags
we carry. Advice trickles in, burrows into

pores: *what you need is diatomaceous earth, stand
the legs of your bed in water. Freeze or throw*

*out your library, the spines of your books
are not immune.* More than once, at 3 a.m.

you jump out of bed, flip on lights to inspect
the mattress. Finding nothing but black specks

of dryer lint, we return to sweat-damp sheets,
as the neon digits of an alarm stitch the diminishing

hours of sleep into my skin. In the morning
we shuffle in silence to make coffee, argue over

how to dispose of the grinds again. A kiss, brief
as a slap, before you're out the door.

Disbelief

We, who do not know if there will ever
be anything but our word against his,

why are our words not midwifed,
laid naked and glistening on our chests
where their cries can be soothed?
Why are they extracted from our throats

with forceps, the stories of our pain
irrevocably dented, every pause
for breath in the recounting seen
a recanting?

It is not enough to say: I am a spotted elm
dying of root rot, my leaves blotched
with blood, green spaces diminishing.

It is not enough to say: I am a Russian nesting doll
whose inner shells have been whittled
into shavings and thrown in the fire.

It is not enough to say: This happened to me.

Paris Memoir with Lines from Neruda's "The Song of Despair"

The memory of you emerges from the night
at Hotel Père-Lachaise after two weeks
of Bordeaux-drunk, hash-fogged

love, all the clotted sap
      of our three months apart
dripping from the drywall. Liquid light drizzled
in figure eights over the Seine's
slow dark wine. So young,

we were green and crowning,
          when suddenly a train
at Gare du Nord swallowed
you whole, folded you into its gunmetal belly.
      I thought, I am *deserted like wharves*

the way young trees are white. It is the hour,
and tender beneath the angry bark,
         I go back to the room where the pillow

still holds the curve of your head.

At dawn, I finally sleep with the sea of you
      rocking in me, whispering,
    Oh, deserted one.

Safety Measures

The door at the end of the long hallway
didn't lead to a room but a ziggurat
of shelves where the sheets and quilts
lived, where I could breathe in
the odours of camphor and lavender,
find a heating pad, my mother's hand-
crocheted poncho, a Hudson's Bay
blanket that could envelop a king-
sized bed with its imperial
tract of white, scratchy wool, acquisition
of my father's youth. His possessions
and hers jockeying for space
to breathe in the confines
of crate-sized chambers. I could climb
up to the top shelf, curl up as though
in a tiny bunk in a ship, a crawl space
from which the world
shrank down. Sometimes I miss it:
the dusty dark, particle board
inches above my face, how the dots
in it merged so they were no longer
dots at all but cells in a living
creature, single-celled throwback
of the Proterozoic. Meanwhile, downstairs
in the kitchen, my parents' sawtoothed
voices escaped, serrated edges scraping
the blanketed air, words that hissed
like steam through fissures
that I tried, for my life, not to hear.

II

Where the Old Road Begins

Just east of the village of Kitseguecla on Highway 16, turn south on the Rocher Deboule Road. After about a kilometre, come to a sand pit on the left, where the old road begins.

—Morgan Hite, "Juniper Creek and Red Rose Mine,"
Northward Magazine

i. *"Mountain Peak at Red Rose, Terrace, BC, Elevation 8,000 feet"*

Nothing in these mountains would ever
suggest convenience stores, gas stations, highways
threading purple veins along the Skeena River.
For ten thousand years, Gitsegukla walking sticks
have pushed this ground beneath us, keeping propeller
spins of vertigo at bay. In our canvas tent, we swig
from a bottle until we drown in sleep, limbs
intertwined more for warmth than love.
Dreams of wild blackberries and foxglove
exhale in musky clouds from our parted lips.
At this altitude, the air thins our words
into lapsed fragments, turning speech into
constellations of syllables that dissolve
into granite dust. Eagles jerk our necks up,
lassoing our dumb gaze. Douglas fir, jack pine
and spruce uphold the sky's ballooning tarp.
So young, we think we can shoot it all—tripods
set up, fingers on shutters, we hold our
position. Lay traps for the perfect postcard
to stumble into our path, trusting dry needles
and bedrock to absorb the bleed.

ii. *"Same as above, only at a higher elevation"*

Nothing in these   highways

                    ten thousand   walking

beneath us, keeping   vertigo

          in our canvas tent   we bottle sleep   for

                    dreams of blackberries

          foxglove
                         clouds   air thins

fragments of speech into

               constellations of granite   lassoing

our dumb gaze

          Douglas fir   jack pine   spruce uphold

          the sky's ballooning tarp

So young we stumble   trusting the needles

          and bedrock
                         absorb   the bleed

iii. *"Cabin at Red Rose Mine"*

We find it half in shadow, as light checker-
boards the buckling porch. Blackened
roof, its boards once nailed together by

split-calloused hands until dark, when mosquitoes
would arrive in drunk militias, thirsty
for a miner's blood. A splintering bench awaits

the next aching figure in this camp of ghosts.
This is a history of incomplete stories,
interrupted by bears or sickness, perhaps

the lack of women—a white man
spearing the myth of vertical power, who'd break
his back out of spite for the voice ringing

in his sun-crisped ears, telling him that somewhere
North or West, he could extract the earth's
metal viscera and in the process, find his own.

And so he slept in this cabin,
bereft of all promised petals, a froth of cold
hunkering in his bones. Awoke at dawn

to make coffee, dunk his head in the creek,
cook breakfast in a cast-iron skillet before
setting out to chisel the mountain's mineral heart.

The Miscreant Speaks

I was born with a caul, a snarl-red bladder of flesh
deemed good luck by the midwife, bartered

for the skull of a deer while I was left
to die. Thrust out of the world

just as I was thrust in. What the books won't tell you
is that I am living now as I write this. Posthumous

gossip doesn't interest me. It hangs, ill-fitted as a skin
the hunters brought back in haste, barely scraped

clean. Throw me back into the well,
back into the womb's sunless estuary, back

into the basalt sea-cave, floored with cobbles, whose
wave-battered walls drip your dazed thirst's last

hope of quench into dark pools below.
You won't even hear a splash.

Hold and Press Eject

Winter dusk comes early, a smear of iodine
on pale skin, the clouds all wisp-smoke, magenta
spiked punch. Your breath feathers the November air
on the way home from school, strapped into
your book bag like a soldier into her parachute,
one hand on the rip cord, ready for deployment.

At home, the phone's been cut off for almost
a month. Sometimes you walk to the pay phone
in the No Frills parking lot to call Michelle
or Jonathan, talk about homework, some new grunge
band, the fucking cliques at school, over the rattle
and bang of shopping carts, collisions of plastic
and steel. One afternoon, you get home

to find your family waiting in the parked car.
Your father gets out, hugs you before you can
see his eyes. *Nobody's dead, he says. The sheriff*
came. Gave us a few hours to pack everything.
He says eviction, and it sounds like *conviction*,
like *eviscerate*, like your mother's choked cough
from the front seat, your sister's yet un-medicated
manic laugh beside you, snow tires grumbling

as your family drives off to the house of an aunt
you haven't seen in years. Soon, the video
stores, cafés, boutiques and small fruit markets
give way to strip malls and gas stations, the gapped
text of suburban erasure. The semi-formal's

only days away, what will you wear,
how will you get back to mid-town, all the way
from Thornhill, is what you want to know.

Khamsin

Nothing in my blue-and-white
flagged past prepared me for the choke
of stories carried on gusts of gritty
wind. During the *khamsin*

handfuls of dust adrift
from the Sinai desert rise in red
storms. We inhale distant dunes
that pass through the checkpoints

of mucous membranes, each granule
a syllable in the name of a village
scrubbed off a map, the earth's
flesh rubbed raw, weeping salt from

the cracks, wounds branded into
memory. At dusk, date palms droop
in dark silhouettes beneath the holy
sky's tourniquet. We breathe in the silt

the land can't abide to keep still.

Gaza under Siege

You are house-sitting—a two-bedroom, air-
conditioned townhouse in Liberty Village, watering
aloe and spider monkey, serving two cups
of dry food a day to a fat white cat named Luca.
Stackable washer and dryer in the hall closet.
You slide open the cool, mirrored doors while
your clothes are kept from shrinking. No laundromat
trips, duffle bag of clothes over your shoulder,
just the nearby shudder of brushed steel machines
doing the labour, while you sit with your laptop
and a glass of cheap Malbec on a couch that's not
yours. King-sized bed in the master too hard, you sleep
on the queen in the guest room: not as firm, just
right. Goldilocks with a key fob, helping yourself
to steel-cut oats and memory foam sleep.
Meanwhile, the death toll of children in Gaza
reaches five hundred. You brush the long-haired cat, sip
your wine, swirling it until it reads as diluted
blood. Read the horror. Remember the sound
of the fireworks in Tel Aviv, on *Yom Ha'atzmaut*,
you were told could just easily have been
rockets. Long ago, at Hebrew day school, you celebrated
that day in May with blue-and-white-frosted cake,
how proud you were that *Eretz Yisrael* was the same
age as your parents. Meanwhile, in Gaza, bodies
and the city's wood and metal bones amass
in baroque jumble, Biblical disarray. On Facebook
you scroll through feeds of loathing, fear culled
from recipes that you once followed—*they brought
this onto themselves, they hate us more than they love*

their own—morsels you can no longer keep down,
no longer digestible nor kosher, which never mattered
before, but for some reason, matters now.

The Intruders

The raccoons have been getting into J's yard again, the newly laid grass
overturned piece by piece by grub-seeking claws. He hates them, curses

them, has waged full-out war, sprinkling the yard with cayenne pepper.
Fantasizes about poisoning the saboteurs of his labour. He has been

hurt, will hurt back. I think of how animals in the wild will defend their
territory,
what nature's choke will drive them to do—in cities, gorge on refuse,

wrestle metal in the jet of night, skip over shingles, scoot across streets
with furtive grace. When he tells me this story I feel as well as hear

it, like the CN Rail trains that rumble behind his apartment on Dupont,
or the sound of something rolling and deep, calm as a decoy that waits

for its enemy, springs to life to ensnare flesh in gleaming machinery.
In bed, my eyes are level with his throat—if his collarbone

were glass, my breath would cloud it. I wonder what would happen
if I ever infringed on his turf, uprooted what lies beneath his composure's

empty field, the snow in the whites of his eyes, hidden caves in the pupils
coiled springs in the snap of his jaw— should I ever trespass

on what he's declared off limits, electric-fenced—
all the defenses accumulated over a life of mishaps.

With Your Permission

I'll do anything in this godalmighty world
If you just let me follow you down.
   —Bob Dylan, "Baby Let Me Follow You Down"

Baby, let me follow you up instead of down
passing joggers breathing snowballs into January air
let me write you a letter on a 1953 Remington typewriter
that won't type the letter S. Baby, let me breathe on your glasses
then rub them with the hem of my shirt. Baby let me
acknowledge our different views when it comes
to Middle Eastern politics before I tongue your chest.
Baby let me tattoo the arcane symbols you dream of
onto my wrists and ankles. Baby, let me drive
with you to old deserted factories where you can photograph
the textures of paint peeling off rusted metal
baby let me take you back to the suburban park
of my childhood, to the hill behind the fence
where we used to watch the trains going by
and my mother would play her guitar & sing
that old freight train folk song. Baby, let me
decipher your heartbeat's semantics. Let me heat up
leftover Phad Thai for breakfast, and eat it naked in bed
baby let me come back to bed and say *I just learned*
I have something in common with the handle
of your toilet, sometimes I like to be held down
baby let me take you back to the night in my nineteenth year
when my sister nearly died of lithium poisoning
let me take you back to my high school bedroom,
slip a pillow between my head and the wall
I bashed it into more than once. Baby let us
grip each other's hands as we cross
these swaying suspension bridges
and keep our eyes on the other side.

New Year's Day

Tonight, the snow drifts
like feathers. It comes
to rest on the roofs

of cars, the sleeping
cattle of these dark,
narrow streets,

and on the streets
themselves,
their pastures,

where feathers fall like
snow, come to
rest on the backs
of cattle

sleeping like parked cars
in dark, frozen pastures,
their streets.

Somewhere, a sidewalk
pushes against
a shovel. A sheet

of paper scrapes
against a pen. Words
erase to clear the page.

After the Argument

In separate rooms of the Vancouver Art Gallery
we examine viscera in oil, acrylic,
wax, and stone Renaissance reverence, or modern
disarray—a litter of organs,

a bloodbath, a shit show. Intestines
pop out of a canvas,
near a column of vertebrae
in bright red yarn and violet

felt, as my own spine feels
. today, no sturdier than a textile
installation, loose threads
unraveling. From a distance, I watch

as you lean over the glass display
where traces of bodily fluids
from a real autopsy splatter. I look,
but cannot touch

you. We find each other again
upstairs beneath the skeleton
of a whale sculpted of white plastic
lawn chairs, as we pass
from innards to inlets—Galliano,

Tsawwassen, Ucluelet, Lasqueti—
salt-sprung music of our new common
geography. Somehow marble softens
into lichen and moss, invisible pine

needles crunch underfoot. Tides ebb, reveal
starfish sleeping amid smoked glass
and seaweed. My arms slip around
your waist as yours slide

over my shoulders. *Let's move on*,
you whisper, though moments pass
before I realize that you mean
> *to the next gallery*.

First Ride of Spring in Toronto

Sunlight unfurls a patchwork quilt over barren
parks, stains them passion fruit dusk, unexpected

as crabapple and whiskey, how the tongue finds its muse
in the most sour of ripenings. Nowhere I'd rather

be than here on my three-speed, navigating the potholes
of Shaw Street, how the pavement blooms

with cracked roses, legacy of the fabled river buried
beneath it though never bullied into submission.

I think of these bodies of concealed water, all the forgotten
reservoirs of blood leaked into this ground, lives

of people born to it for millennia, the waterways that carried
them, an apothecary of names I want to recite, eyes

closed, forehead pressed to marble monuments: Lake Iroquois,
the *Cobechenonk*, Garrison Creek,

Taddle Creek, Castle Frank Brook. The city's
jagged veins lie translucent in their concrete graves.

After Watching *Before Sunset*

Sometimes, I hate Paris, all the longing
it extorts in the unlikeliest of moments,
a rain dance bringing flash floods
              instead of solace.

This film's one long take, light
of early evening butter-soft
over Julie Delpy's herringbone
skin. She plays a simple waltz
on her guitar in her fifth floor

walk-up, herbal tea and plant-filled
loft, a calico cat sleeping on the windowsill,
bookshelves lined with Plath,
Miller, Nin, and Sartre: the place
I once thought was mine
for the having.

When she puts on a Nina Simone
record for Ethan Hawke
in that final scene—*Just in time,
  you found me*—Fuck.

She quotes from her journals.

I want to caution her: there's poison
in the ink of old documents—
a boy wrote my name in Irish
calligraphy, beside a haiku
about my hair: *like poplars in wind.*

My youth preserved between covers
warped by rain. Run your hands along
the book's edges. Its spine was
always crooked.

Elegy for G. Harrison

You're asking me will my love grow
I don't know, I don't know
—G.H., "Something"

I see you as a boy, onstage in Hamburg, sweaty-faced, hands
sliding automatically over strings (*frothing*

at the mouth, as you later put it), Chuck Berry riffs &
rockabilly licks all night, till the last pill wears off. There's

more to pop. Around a sticky table in the Reeperbahn
later, swilling dark beer with the boys & your new stripper

girlfriends, did you dream of Ed Sullivan, of "Tomorrow
Never Knows," the Maharishi, Ravi Shankar,

aromas of ganja & sandalwood rising up through a sitar, your new
appendage? That you might one day be canonized, Saint

George & the dragon you fought until your lungs one day
capitulated, clotted with tar, black as Liverpool

smoke. There the cancer bloomed, wild as young
reeds. Now I confess it wasn't you I loved, but the way

the sunlight first swung into my room when
something first swelled in my blood.

Outside /In

after photographs at the "Outsiders" exhibit at the Art Gallery of Ontario, May 2016

They call themselves Selma, Doris,
Nancy, Louise—when they are not Fred
Bill, Frank, Louis—birth names itch

like rayon, demand pulling away
from the chafe. Chest hair visible beneath
the lingerie they can safely wear here:

a robin's-egg peignoir, eggplant silk
scarf, bras built like wartime airplanes
they once might have piloted

as Fred, Bill, Frank, Louis, writing letters
to sweethearts with names like Selma, Doris,
Nancy, Louise. I want to join them

in these photographs, dance
to some syrupy Henry Mancini instrumental,
the Supremes or Chubby Checker, at Casa Susana

in the Catskills, clink highball glasses,
drink Manhattans and vermouth
martinis. I want to ask them how, in the age

of my parents' youth, while my father
was a peacock display of teenage
masculinity, while my mother

awkwardly carried the weight
of her beehive, they found the courage
to find each other, knew the secret

handshake, slipped into their true skins.

The Night Swimmers

Montfort, Quebec, 1996, deep spring. Foliage pungent. Midnight journey to the lake, clothes come off. Nineteen years old, first shock of air on exposed skin, strange newness of warm wind in and over and between everything. Simon says, It's so dark I can't see my own member. We step carefully over pebbles, sharp twigs, combat black flies swarming for a midnight binge. Craig, quiet Christian drummer in Simon's band, hangs back by the tress, fully clothed, watching. First shock of water as I go in ankle deep and shriek. Next splash and Chloe's in. She shrieks, howls, laughter deeper than boreal lakes. Then Kelly. Simon wades and dives. My gooseflesh rises. Deep breath and plunge, cold water biting. I am underwater in womb silence, blood silence, suspended before the break to surface. Pedaling blue-black cool water beneath a floodlight moon, a million billion trillion stars above us. Chloe yells, Spread your legs in and out, it feels great. After, we lie on the empty road on our backs, share a joint as the planet spins. Pavement holds daytime heat. It's safe, Chloe says. No one ever this way, not at this time. Night curves its two cupped palms around us. Walking back to the house, a car speeds down the road from where we have just risen. In silence, we marvel at our unharmed flesh, newly minted, cresting.

Poem for Baba Yaga, with Line from Philip Levine

She in her empty room in heaven
grazes the sinuous fog, almost animal it its contagion
A growl somersaults in her throat, comes out a sigh
What draws me to her, this crone, this angel
on this cryogenic winter's morning, a plum darkness
my partner still sleeps in, while I stumble through cobwebs
to turn on the kettle? Could it be the dream of
my grandmother I had last night, where she appraised
my tattoos with cool amusement as they drifted
across my skin like cloud formations, sweeping shadows
over forested landscape? Could it be the archway
I am forever approaching, but never passing under, always
a fixture of the mind's moonscape?

How to Write a Hanukkah Poem

1.
Choose your preferred spelling of Hanukkah,
from the seven or eight available. Assemble
your arsenal: dreidls your father would show off
by spinning upside down. Latkes. Paper towels
to soak up the grease from latkes, paper bags
to soak up the grease from the paper towels, candles
that will melt and harden in the menorah, scraped

out next year with the tip of a steak knife, hard flakes
of coloured wax. Whatever you do, don't call
the menorah the *hanukkiah*, the proper word
you learned long ago in Hebrew school:
it will sound too specific, too accurate, above-
board. You will alienate most people, or worse,
charm them with your exoticness.

2.
Subvert. Make dreidl games dirty. Strip off clothing
if the dreidl lands on the letter *gimmel*. Truth
is daring. Make "space latkes" that will get you
higher than the most mystical of cabbalists,
taste the colours of candles bursting with sweet

liquid. Snort lines off pages of the Talmud. Forget
about inviting distant relatives who always tell
you what they prefer to do. None of this will give
you joy, only stories to display like dark ribbons
on your chest, a catalogue of scars for the shocked listener.

3.

Write. Invoke the light. Invoke the hand that holds
the *shamash*, moving from light to light. Invoke
small haloes around each candle, pancake moons
around the heads of gaunt-faced Russian icons.

Invoke more light, the light that ushers you through
December's dark, the light that leaves nothing
in its wake that is cold or unkind.

All the Living He Has Left

for C.T.

You never go to bed as a 21-year-old, thinking the boy
    who sleeps beside you will not live to see his fortieth

birthday, knowing that more than half his life has passed
    by the point at which you enter it. All the living he has

left in him, he will do as a young man, even as his hair,
    its black and purple tips gelled up into stiff waves, begins

to thin. The morning after you take him home from
    a Queen Street Goth club, your black fishnets and his,

both smelling of beer and Djarum clove cigarettes,
    catching each other in Celtic knots beneath

your futon on the cold unswept floor, you never think
    fifteen years later, you'll be reading the words *Devoted*

husband, father, son, and brother about him on the Internet.
    A sudden end, as ends usually are, unlike endings,

which stretch long and thin before the final break. He pulls
    on his leather pants, his fourteen-hole Docs,

his long black jacket. You walk him to the door
    and once he's gone, you make your coffee,

bring it out to the balcony, notice winter's naked
    branches beginning to green.

You Were So Brave To Hold a Stranger

for my sister, Caroline

We signed you out on a clipboard, as if we had
to rent you. Outside the hospital, where the gravel
paths sloped into green, all the grass precise, immaculate
in its order, you started to run, feet turned outward

with a puffin's uneven gait, wrists flapping
by your sides as if trying to fly out of your fog,
break from lithium's mustard haze. When I paused
on a bench, you sat down and put your arms around

me, rocking back and forth, all the while never
refusing to answer the voices you gently cocked
your head to hear. Your dilated pupils so volcanic
black I had to strain to see the Atlantic

grey-blue behind them. Words I couldn't catch
spilled out of you in one unbroken lava flow.
I remembered in kindergarten, how you protected me
from the school bus bullies who'd reach

from the seat behind us to grab the toque
off my head. You got it back for me every time.
How could I have known then I would
one day be held tight against your large, soft body,

lulled by your mumblings, the inchoate song
of the ocean locked in the conch, before
it became a memory of itself. You were
so brave to hold me—now, a complete

stranger to you—or perhaps you saw me
as someone you'd once met in a dream, a person
you would have loved and protected
if you had grown up together.

III

Unauthorized

I was born fully clothed in chartreuse satin, which covered my feathers and scales.

I drank the song of the sea through my mother's oyster milk, licked the snow-capped teeth of mountains.

I was raised in a time when wolves recited Homeric epics to the full buttered moon.

I played second trombone for the demons' philharmonic, conducted lightning for the Archangels Symphony Orchestra.

I fried handfuls of crushed stars in a pan of midnight oil.

I held my breath for forty days and forty nights, swam all the way to Atlantis.

Guest, Unannounced

You fly out of the darkness at me,
twisting open the tin sky.
—Anne Michaels

As sleep carves its name into tree bark,
next to mine, I see you, not as you are
now—greying stubble, a dad's polo

shirt stretched over slight paunch—but as I knew you
at twenty-three, an Israeli Jim Morrison in *sharwal*
pants, *kafkafim* on your bare, shuffling feet

who once photographed me nude with a tiny Buddha
on my chest. You, with your guitar
slung over your back, a satchel in polished walnut,

songs and poems floating from your lips
in rings lighter than the smoke of the banana leaf
cheroots you'd brought back from Burma.

You return to me, with your smile and your
one false, perfect tooth. The time you
wouldn't just let me go back into my uncle's house

outside Jerusalem on the night of our first date
without charging after me for one more
kiss, at the moment you knew you could outdo

the last. Tonight, you stir the molecules
behind my eyelids, leaving in the spaces
between them the strokes of all the letters

we wrote: the ones I kept, the ones I left behind.

Transplant within Vancouver

In a dream I cut my tongue, tasted
blood as I awoke. Even indoors, stones away
from the Pacific's hypothermic blue lip, salt
laces the air, lingers on the rim of a wine
glass long past its rinsing. By day, I walk
in the shade of trees whose branches sway

within feathery sleeves, foliage of bohemian
nymph, magnolias in full bloom behind
poodle-clipped hedges. I walk along
West 4th, past the yoga studios, the juice bars
and sushi joints. I practice my Downward Dog
but my back won't go straight. I don't tan

well, care much for quinoa. My home street
in East Van feels a better fit: where there's
grit, there's depth. Cheap coffees, slices
of pizza at Uncle Fatih's at Broadway
and Commercial, the swirl in the grain
of the rain coast's washed-up wood, as

glass and chrome displace arbutus
and Sitka spruce. Where I live, our clothes
dry where others can see them, our secrets flap
their woven tongues. Outside, crows gather
to consider abandoned crusts on sidewalks, not far
from the thrift stores I'm known to haunt.

Here, at Stef's place, two bridges over
near Kits Beach, I sweep out the sand
the dog tracks in until I relent. I let it stay.

To My New Grey Hairs

after Jacob Scheier

I find you springing askew from my scalp,
bent, wispy as if afraid, growing in a climate
that might prove hostile to your survival. What I feel
is not a fear of age but the beginning
of an age of fear: crow's feet around my eyes
writing a language of history where once the skin
stretched hospital corner-taut, the gravity of breasts
growing heavier into season. Beneath a vanity's
bright lights I go searching of more of you, find you gleaming
near the temples, behind an ear's shadowed corner.
Near the hairline, one long strand of your magic
floss. In ten, fifteen years, will my dark hair be
an expired passport's faded stamp? I see you waiting
in silver stasis to glimmer at night, when I'm sleeping
with my lover, whose cheek or forehead might touch you
in the night without knowing he is brushing up
against the woman I not yet am.

To a Lump

I

Nameless before the ultrasound, you lurk
in my breast, a centimeter or so from
the nipple, a pit lodged in a windpipe,
all smoldering acorn quietness. I push down,
trying to make out your contours—what is the size
and shape of the weapon sprung and loaded,
what is the weight of the stone in the snowball
a young boy throws in Deptford, hitting
the pastor's pregnant wife? Try not to worry,
the doctor tells me, it's most likely benign. Just
swallow these nails without scratching your throat.
Try to relax beneath the noose whose sinews
I have just placed around your chipped porcelain
neck. Still, knowing you are in there, but not
knowing who you are, or what you will do to me,
I cup your vessel, playing host to a guest in a ski mask.
All I can do is offer you tea and clean linens, remember
to caution you that the bathroom light's gone out
and you'll have to use the lamp by the sink,
ask you about your origins, how long you'll be
in town for. Perhaps some day, on a busy street,
we'll see each other again, you'll know me,
though I won't know you, and you'll thank
me for the hospitality, and I'll just say, *It was nothing.*

Simple Present

after Robert Bly

Is the way we move antithetical
to breathing? The heart is a finite muscle
of blood and music.

You walk alongside me over
bleached concrete. Your hands fly
and your voice turns the heads of pedestrians
who disguise themselves as molecules.
What is good, is good.
But it doesn't last.

How can we laugh if our lips refuse
to part? In rush hour, it all comes down
to hushed voices, thin air.

Make a sound. Make a sound
that sounds like something
other than the muffled grunt of
Sorry or *Excuse me*, make
love or promises you'll keep
for a good, long time.

Letter

tasting blood on your tongue
does not shock me
   —Leonard Cohen, "Letter"

Unknowingly, you choose to recite the poem
that haunts me most. I listen as if
hearing these words being written
for the first time, as if my ear
were pressed to the grain of the oak table
in a Montreal library or cafe, fifty-
some-odd years ago, where the prophet
Leonard drinks coffee, sits with his notebook
and ashtray, both near overflowing, and my hair
gets smoky so I put it up in a bun before
I return to this bathtub in East Vancouver,
where your damp, curly head lies in the crook
of my shoulder, over breastbone, close to,
I might add, but not over the heart. Chagall
would paint us as two already drowned lovers
ascending to saffron clouds over a mosaic
of blue and copper *shtetl* rooftops
reflected in our pupils, while in the
gutter below, a red-bearded fool wrests
love songs, out of spite as much as mercy,
from his blood-caked violin.

She Comes Out of Church

or does it come out of her, as she imagines it
sometimes, steeple and slanted roof poking through
blouse, neck-hole and sleeves. Seven years old,
her body lighter than its shadow. Head
thrown back, she runs down the wooden
steps. If the wind were a colour, it would be
the same green as everything that appears
in sunlight spots beneath eyelids, moss, vermilion,
the dark shade they call hunter. Skipping over
grass and a gravel path, her hand
seeks out her father's, finds and holds, a warm glove
she slips on, fits into. She hears her name,
turns to see her parents' mouths wide open, hear
their surprised laughter, look up into the stranger's
face, the man whose hand she's grasped
in error. Years later, she will recall this, the way shame
rose in prickles beneath her skin, reached places
she had no names for. The first, but not the last man
she would mistakenly grasp and let go.

After the End of the Light's Sabbatical

I want to go back to that place, the two-storey cabin
on the edge of the pond clotted with algae and chemical
run-off from the mansion next door. I want to return
to that afternoon in early April, Canada geese breaking
V-formation to fly side-by-side in moving clotheslines
overhead, wings scything the chill-struck sky,
their voices cracking like the hoots of adolescent boys
on their way home from school. I want to go back
to that hinge-day, the fulcrum
between seasons, back to the empty house across the pond
from my friend's house in the hillside. Touch
its fresh, unpainted walls, climb the stairs
to the A-frame attic, infused with cedar and linseed,
where the milkweed light of these lengthening days
scours the dark from shadowed corners. I want
this day of walking with hands in pockets—no purse
straps clawing into muscle, no phone, no conveyor
belts of concrete underfoot, no skyscrapers
or towers bayoneting the horizon's glazed canvas.
I want to feel how the earth gives beneath my mud-
coated boots, like the give of a heavy stone that finally
moves after hours of work in the cold, breathe
in the smells of mulch and thaw, like the smells of sex
and sweat, marvel at the remaining patches of snow
hugging the boggy land: their ragged slate
edges topstitched like lace, so delicately wrought I marvel
at their artistry, at the way they scatter like archipelagos
over spreading seas of green, as silver flake
by flake they surrender, they melt into flow.

A Day So Ordinary It Barely Brushes Our Skin

The highway glides out from beneath us, all mirrors
and seal's pelt gloss. Sleep and rain arrive together, sheets

of water silver the taupe landscape, braiding in the rain's
tapping nails on the double-decker sunroof. Minutes or hours

later, I awaken on my love's shoulder. Halfway between Montreal
and Toronto, we straddle embankments, balloon in nether-space,

far from where our footing's apt to trust. Only six months since
that first snowy night, corner of Bloor and Dufferin—we kissed

in the cold for half an hour while I missed bus after bus, delaying
eventual rift, splinter of impending split. Now, we're on board

with the drift that comes with sealing ourselves in our own
private worlds, returning at times from our naps and music

and books to find each other again, hips relieved of magnetic
siren songs, learning their own ways. A day I wouldn't think

remarkable, and remember precisely because of that.

Mirror Image

for Nathan, 1980-2005

More than a year after your death, I think
of bulls pulling the weight of stars in heaven,
stubborn suck of constellations, joining us
together: friends born in May, three years
and two days apart, fixed signs
of the Earth. I took your word for this, astrology
never my strong suit. Your Italian-Northern
Ontario roots, my Toronto-Montreal-Jewish
intertwining as they splintered underground.

You could not contain your rage over my leaving
out the Saran Wrap, dishes abandoned in the valley
of the sink. A conversation outside your bedroom
waking you, after a double shift at the bistro.
Such a diva, I dismissed you. Diva, how I miss you.

How you worshipped Diamanda Galas, whose music
I said reminded me of cats trapped in a violin.
Your passion for Kate Bush and Bette Midler.
How you said, *I love cock.* I loved that you could say
this—you, who grew up in a northern mining
town—how easily you'd speak of those men
who held you captive, with their easy grins, the palpable
warmth of them.

Once, you cut my hair, a mirror propped up
on the table, and I could see your hands working.
I watched you, each precise shearing
and fraying, each swan dive of your arm, the layers
you added as layers fell away.

They say I should forgive myself for not
saving you, for not returning your phone call soon
enough—perhaps the last one you made. You are
with me still, above or behind me, whispering,
These split ends really need to go.

Absinthe Makes the Heart Grow Fungus

You find yourself at a bar in Prague,
caramelizing sugar on a heated spoon
that will dissolve into emerald wine.
Made with wormwood: you think
of foliage, soil, and shit, gummy tubes
of pink flesh surfacing after rain.

After the next round, you're clutching
the throat-feathers of an eagle flying
into a black sun until the lighter's corrugated metal
bites into your thumb, then heating the next
spoonful of sugar over the glass
(does it really make the medicine go down
or does it does it make it rise up?),

helium head getting lighter
while the fire spreads down and out
through heart and belly, eating
everything in its path.

Watermarked

after The Morning After The Deluge, *J. M. W. Turner (c. 1843)*

After the flood, we roast doves over rusted
barrels, lick the sap of olive branches
from each other's throats, though our hands
      still bleed from their puncture wounds.

      We squat in cold museums, deserted condominium
showrooms stockpiled with each day's forage
and plunder. My hunger, a knotted tuber, grows eyes
in my belly's dark burlap. You lock

          your tongue in confinement.
My words gather in bundles I can't hold
much longer. To speak of what's been lost, the oilcloth
I stuff my own mouth with. In your sleep, I hear you

      call out for the woman before me. By day,
you chloroform my questions with a single look.
I finger her ashes, a fine coating over your skin.
So much water everywhere, enough to quench

      a Sahara-sized thirst, yet we can
scarcely drink it with our stomachs' consent—
no first-born to use as currency for something cleaner.

So much water swamping cities, devouring
expanses of sprawl. Waves higher than Babel
crash over bank towers, whole islands bright wrecks
      in the ocean. Highways spill concrete entrails,

　　　　billboards glint their drowned teeth
through white churning pools
where the light whisks all the shadows
　　　of the world into blue-gold silence and froth.

Taking Stock: A Cento

There are things you can't reach. An old man
recalls an antique joke.

I want to say,
Every day I feel my fate

in what I cannot fear—it's shining there now,
a thing

like a woman & man who have lived
in wildlife. Comb the beach for the perfect shell.

No release without first being bound
in a series of sharp ghosts without stories.

Maybe it's the dead, tender and tough
shapes in sea-mist, half-nothing

and everything, all this: this ocean, this world.

Tango Lesson

After a history lesson, crash course in Buenos Aires
a hundred years before our time, we begin

at last. You gently place my arm over yours, my hand
on your shoulder, our bodies distant enough

to have an invisible body between us—this is open embrace,
you explain, *abrazo abierto*. We dare not dance in *abrazo cerrado*,

where our chests would nearly touch—I'm not single-
minded enough about learning these moves to unlock

what I fear might spill out, should I let myself fall
into your hazelnut voice—so rich, so deep, I might never

want to leave it. You teach me the new skill of following,
though your lead feels less like control and more

like stewardship, carving swans of negative space
that stretch their graceful necks along the diagonals

of our bodies. We're in a conversation of pauses
and advances. I step too soon, but you are eminently patient,

your large hand over mine, poised mid-air, a paper crane
mid-flight. As you shift your weight from side to side, I wait,

trying to sense, as you instruct me, which way we are going,
and for a moment, I have the chance to look at you not

looking at me, your grey-green eyes fixed above my head.
On the small of my back, your warm hand—

a breathing orchid, cupped flame.

Please Don't Go, We'll Eat You Up, We Love You So

for Maurice Sendak ("Where the Wild Things Are")

i.
Summer of '35. The monsters in your
Bensonhurst closet go, *Look at him,*
not a little pischer anymore,
he's grown so big! Uncle Schmuel
kisses you

though you're eight-and-three-quarters.
Auntie Rosie's bosom is a bosom,
beige silk sleeveless blouses

salt-stained beneath whitefish
biceps, onion sweat and perfume
of moist cleavage she pulls you into.

Marbled yellowing teeth threaten
to tear into your flesh and devour you
with groans of guttural Yiddish.

ii.
On the way home from school,
the Horowitz boys corner you
in the alley, spritz lisp-spray through
their teeth into your eyes.

They straddle your chest, mash
your face with ham-hock

fists, hungry for your jaw's
soft pulp. They call you *faigele*

and you are not sure what
this means, only know
it is something you're not
supposed to be.

You don't know that years
from now, in Greenwich Village,
you'll find other boys, the ones
who will spoon you on sagging
mattresses in cold-water flats,

smoking, drinking coffee
brewed on your single hot-plate
after love. Boys whose bodies
you will devour
with groans of guttural Yiddish.

iii.
At night you shut your eyes, sail
into the hairy-starred
ocean night, your breath
a silver diaphanous shroud

in the onyx chilled air, and the sea
sways like armies of arms holding
up a bridegroom's chair

to the high bleating notes
of Klezmer clarinets. Dizzy, open-
mouthed, you land in the tangled
forest, where the wild things

sing the world into being, scoop
you up into shaggy embrace
and you hope to God they won't let go.

Blind Date

Barely a pint in, words slacken
and die in my mouth, as the mind pedals
its rusty unicycle up another goddamned
hill, in the rain. I search for artifacts

to inquire about: an unusual ring, a concert
t-shirt for some metal band I've never heard
of. Without established ground, we dust for stories
while trying not to cross the yellow

tape or walk on the wet cement, going
instead for what's safe and easy. What surfaces
are not questions but careful unmasking
of doubts that cling to the lungs, mitigate

breathing. We pretend to listen as we plot
our next move, then the subject's
dropped and before you know it we're back
to the weather, how everyone's getting sick

these days, even in the middle of July.

What the Night Brings into Morning

When Chloe said that death is a cleansing, I thought
she meant for the dead. That you were now cold
and pure—death disinfected you from all the tubers of life.
But she meant for us. In the basement of a Montreal
synagogue, ripe with the smell of your absence,
I studied the tiles, boiled chicken-beige, thought of
hospitals, elementary school classrooms, all the ways
we devise to shrink endless stretches of time.
I sat there that day, with Kelly and Simon and Chloe
and Ian, and Kelly's friend, Imad. We talked about
that time we all went to Café Sarajevo for a night
of Django jazz, how we lounged on red velvet sofas, all the cigarettes
and pitchers of beer we went through, even those of us
who didn't smoke or drink. All we were missing
was a hookah. I thought of you sitting
on the opposite sofa, your curly black hair, your eyes
a charcoal you could smudge for the contour of shadow
below a cheekbone, nimbus clouds before heavy rain,
like that night in my dorm room when you came upstairs
after walking me home from the bar. I made tea.
You read me your poems, which had earnest questions
about war I nodded over, looking away as I wondered
if our conversation would finish in bed.
Six months later, at your memorial, your mother,
who never knew me, embraced me, and all I could think
to tell her was how much you loved poetry.

Tonight the Moon

Nobody understands how I could have left you,
Vancouver: cherry blossom petals soaking in spring

        fountains, mountains reflected in puddles,
        green cloud-splash

eye of Magritte, clear turquoise. For over a year

      I drowned in drizzle
mist-choked, until my skin pruned, until my drab clay

          tongue grew slack with calm

Tonight, in Toronto, the moon is that thing
I picture when I hear
         the word moon, pulling me
         by my hair

back to this moment, this city, where my roots thrust
into lush cement

This soft September evening,
    I bicycle through Kensington

      past the shuttered cafes and vintage stores,

narrow streets dark and sputtering
beneath my wheels

past Toronto Western Hospital
where I was born

        as two coasts fold and meet
corner to corner, palm to palm

Patrilineal

i.

Lilac trees bind me to a past we both imagine:
your Montreal boyhood, from street gang in Snowdon

to the suburban garden in Côte Saint-Luc
that your mother planted, hoping it would not be

uprooted, having lost three children before you,
her eldest, were born, not to mention another life

in Poland. Legend has it at twenty you danced around
a campfire, catapulting stars into a glass

of whiskey. Leapt over flames to land in a pretty girl's
lap, marrying her six months later against her parents'

wishes. Along the walk of your family's split-level
on Robinson, squat geometry of post-war progress,

pale amethyst blossoms released their fragrance, each
bloom a private world, a cell, a moment in a lived life, defined.

ii.

Visiting Toronto, you embarrass me at a café, disgruntled
by barista linguistics, smirking as you remark

on our young server's androgyny. Later, you commandeer
the pepper mill from a surprised waiter to grind it

over your own plate, as the ticker tape of your heroic transgressions
keeps ticking into the night. My own sentences, barely

a few words in, guillotined as your parallel stories arrive
in quick succession. Your life over-writing my own.

iii.
and when I stand before you, questioning the lens
through which the world flattens itself in your presence,

I'm just choosing to take offense again, like the teenager
you once called bitchy, strident. *Women's libber.*

Father, you taught me well how to stand
my ground, descend a rocky slope sideways,

one foot crossing over the other, as if dancing the horah.
Trained me, as a girl of ten, to make a good

fist, throw a punch straight from the elbow
then slam it, bare-knuckled, into your open palm.

iv.
Before you leave for the airport, you hold me
tight. I cannot see, but know your eyes are tearing

like mine. I wait for the breath I will exhale
once you're gone, when I can go back

to missing and not-missing you, a room
I know so well I can find my way in the dark.

v.
Continents apart, there are words
in the spaces between our words.

We don't speak of the past, but of botanicals:
the lilacs in full bloom in our distant cities,

the heat that makes them wilt,
the rain that startles them into growing.

Notes

"Inscription" and "A Day So Ordinary It Barely Brushes Our Skin" are for Stéphane.

"Long Exposure" started as a response to collaborative poem that I wrote with Anthony Stechyson in one of Stuart Ross's "Poetry Boot Camp" workshops.

"Fragments of Tel Aviv": The word *Arsim* is the plural form of the Hebrew word "ars," a derogatory Hebrew slang term for the stereotype of a low-class young man of Mizrahi origin (Mizrahim are Israeli Jews who immigrated to Israel from Muslim countries, and their descendants). —Wikipedia contributors, "Ars" (slang), *Wikipedia*, wikipedia.org, (accessed September 27, 2016).

"Where the Old Road Begins": The titles of the sections, "Mountain Peaks at Red Rose," "Same as above, only at higher elevation," and "Cabin at Red Rose Mine," come from the captions written on the backs of old photographs I discovered at a yard sale, which served as the inspiration for these poems.

"New Year's Day" is for David Bowie (RIP).

"After the Argument" is partially an ekphrastic poem, inspired by the *Visceral Bodies* exhibition at the Vancouver Art Gallery, February 6-May 16, 2010.

"Elegy for G. Harrison": Certain details in the poem, including the line "stripper girlfriends," come from interviews with George Harrison and Paul McCartney, as recalled in Dave Lifton's article, "The History of the Beatles' First Hamburg Show," on ultimateclassicrock.com.

"To a Lump": The line "a stone in a snowball / a young boy throws in Deptford, hitting the pastor's pregnant wife" is a reference to Robertson Davies' novel *Fifth Business*.

"Absinthe Makes the Heart Grow Fungus": The title comes from graffiti spotted in a bathroom in Kensington Market.

"Please Don't Go, We'll Eat You Up, We Love You So": The title of this poem comes from one of the most beloved books of my childhood, the great Maurice Sendak's *Where the Wild Things Are*. The poem was in part inspired by Stacy Conradt's article "Ten Things You Might Not Know About Maurice Sendak."

"Taking Stock: A Cento": Lines in the poem come from Evelyn Lau, Kate Braid, Theodore Roethke, and others.

"What the Night Brings into Morning" is for Oren G. (RIP).

"Patrilineal": The line "Your life over-writing my own" was suggested by Stéphane Savoie.

Acknowledgments

Sincere thanks to the editors of the journals where some of these poems, or earlier versions of them, have appeared: *Canthius*, *The Literary Review of Canada*, *Crab Creek Review*, *(parenthetical)*, *The Puritan*, *The Malahat Review*, *The Scrivener Creative Review*, *lichen literary journal*, and *The Rock Salt Plum Review*. "Where the Old Road Begins" was longlisted for the 2015 CBC Poetry Prize. I gratefully acknowledge the support of the Toronto Arts Council in the creation and completion of this book.

My deepest gratitude to the entire team at Tightrope Books: to my publisher, Jim Nason, for his faith in this book; Heather Wood, for all her helpfulness, generosity, and sense of humour throughout this process, and the book designer, David Jang. Thanks to my incredible mother, Janice Colman, for allowing me to use her luminous painting for the cover.

Huge thanks to my friend and editor, Jacob Scheier, for all the keen insights, brilliant editorial advice, encouragement, and guidance. Thanks to Stuart Ross and Robin Richardson for incredibly helpful feedback and suggestions on many of these poems, and to Jessica Burnquist, who read an early draft of the manuscript and first suggested the title.

Many of the poems in this collection were workshopped with the Plasticine Collective poets, to whom I am deeply grateful, especially Susie Petersiel Berg, Lisa Young, and Michael Fraser. My thanks go out to the talented and gracious poets of Pandora's Collective in Vancouver. I am grateful to Nancy and Marty Kurylowicz of Guelph, Ontario, and to Small Pond Arts in Prince Edward County, for providing beautiful spaces in which to write. Thanks to Kelly Norah Drukker, for over two decades of friendship, poetry exchanges over countless cups of herbal tea, and support. My love and gratitude to my closest friends, and most importantly to my parents, Janice Colman and A. Stephan Richter, and my sister, Caroline, for never failing to believe I had this book in me.

Lastly, to my wonderful partner, Stéphane, first reader of so many poems: thank you for your enduring love, your superhuman patience, and for always having my back. I am a better writer and person for it.

About the Author

PHOTO: Matthew Burpee

Lisa Richter's work has appeared in or is forthcoming in *The Puritan*, *Minola Review*, *The Malahat Review*, *Canthius*, and *lichen*, amongst others, and has been longlisted for the CBC Poetry Prize. *Closer to Where We Began* is her first full-length collection of poetry. Lisa lives and teaches English in Toronto.